Miss Hull

DECISIC, ᵕᵕ,
DECISIONS

Retold by Becca Heddle

Series Advisor Professor Kimberley Reynolds

Illustrated by Jun Cen

15214

Letter from the Author

I love telling stories – don't you? Especially on a long walk. When you start getting tired, a good story can keep you going. The stories I like best make me laugh or make me think.

The stories you're about to read all come from different continents. They make you think because each one features a dilemma – a seemingly impossible situation. In *The Circle of Chalk* and *Clever Gretchen*, the characters are trapped by a dilemma. One is solved in a dramatic way, while the other one is rather funny.

The Three Daughters is different. It is one of hundreds of 'dilemma tales' from African countries, where the question is left to us to solve. The idea is to get a discussion going. Now that sounds like it would help on a long walk ...

Becca Heddle

Clever Gretchen

Once upon a time, in a country covered with woods and farmland, there lived a clever young woman called Gretchen. Gretchen was in love with a young man called Jacob. The story starts with him.

Jacob lived with his mother in a little cottage in the woods. Gretchen was the daughter of the mayor, who lived in a fine house built of stone. Everyone said the mayor would never let his daughter get married. But whenever Jacob and Gretchen passed in the street, she gave him a dazzling smile.

Jacob couldn't stop thinking about Gretchen. He loved her and he was determined to marry her.

One night, Jacob talked to his mother about it.

'Oh Jacob, you're a hopeless romantic!' She shook her head. 'There is no way Gretchen's father will let her marry you. What do you have to offer a mayor's daughter?'

5

But Jacob told his mother how Gretchen smiled at him. In the end, she agreed to go and talk to the mayor.

The next morning, Jacob's mother put on her cleanest apron and headed off to the mayor's house.

Of course, the mayor did not want Gretchen to marry Jacob.

He said, 'My Gretchen must marry a man of great skill. I have always said ... ' He paused and twiddled his moustache. 'Yes, I've always said he must be an excellent hunter ... Can your son shoot the whiskers off a rabbit, without hurting it at all? If so, tell him to come and show me. Then I'll think about it.'

Well, Jacob was very good with his bow, but this was an impossible task! His mother went home and told him what Gretchen's father had said.

'I'm already the best shot in the area. If anyone can do it, I can,' Jacob declared. And he went out into the woods to practise.

Jacob's mother shook her head. Her poor son was so sick with love, he just didn't understand the situation. The mayor would never let him marry Gretchen.

Jacob walked through the woods. He spotted a rabbit and aimed an arrow at it – then he lowered his bow and sighed. He was a skilled hunter, but what Gretchen's father wanted was impossible!

Just then, a stranger stepped out from behind a tree. He was very tall and was dressed all in red.

'What's the matter, Jacob?' said the stranger – as if he and Jacob were friends.

Jacob didn't like the look of this man in red. But somehow, he couldn't resist. He found himself telling him the whole story.

'You know, I can help you with the shooting thing,' said the stranger, stroking his chin. 'Would you like to make a deal?'

Jacob felt hope flood through him. He nodded his head.

'Pass me your bow,' the stranger said. 'I'll see what I can do to make it work better.'

Jacob handed over his bow, wondering what the stranger would do. The tall man in red lifted it up and blew along the string.

'There!' he said, passing the bow back.
'Try it out. Then we'll discuss the payment.'

Jacob took out a new arrow and lifted
his bow. He aimed and fired at a rabbit.
Twang! The rabbit scooted away, scared
but unharmed – and there were
its long whiskers on
the ground!

'Good shot,' said the stranger, with an unpleasant smile. 'Now for our deal. Your bow will keep its power. But after ten years you must come away with me. Then you'll be my servant forever.'

'All right,' said Jacob. He was examining his bowstring, not really listening.

'Just sign this contract,' said the stranger. He held out a piece of paper covered in writing, and a pen dripping with red ink.

But then Jacob thought about Gretchen. He knew how clever she was. She would never agree to a deal without making sure she got exactly what she wanted.

So he said, 'I want to add two things to the contract. For the next ten years, you will work for me and come whenever I call. And at the end of the ten years, I will go with you, unless ... ' He stopped and thought.

This was hard. 'Unless I can ask you a question which you cannot answer.'

The stranger looked at Jacob coolly,
then flicked a speck of dust off his fine red
clothes. He shook the contract and the extra
words appeared on it. 'Sign here,' he said.

Jacob signed, and the stranger tucked
the contract back into his sleeve. Then he
reached into his pocket. He gave Jacob a tiny
whistle made of bone.

'Blow this whenever you need me,' he
said. 'I'll come and do what you wish. And
ten years from today, I'll come for you.'

Before Jacob could say goodbye,
the stranger vanished among the trees.

The next morning, Jacob picked up his
bow and arrows and went off
to see the mayor.

'Well?'
said the
mayor,
looking
down his
nose.

'I would
like to marry
Gretchen.'
Jacob swallowed
nervously. 'I
can shoot as
well as
you require.'

The mayor's eyebrows shot up. 'Prove it,' he barked. He bustled Jacob off the doorstep and looked at the sky. A magpie was flying overhead.

'Shoot at that magpie,' said the mayor. 'I want just one feather off its tail.'

Jacob fitted an arrow in his bow and aimed at the bird. He loosed off the arrow. *Twang!* The magpie flew on, and a single tail feather fluttered down. It landed right at the mayor's feet.

Gretchen smiled at Jacob from her window.

'Impressive!' said her father. 'But I have always said that Gretchen's husband must be, um ... skilled at farming. Bring me a plough that can move on its own – without a horse or a man. Oh, and it has to plough three furrows at once, not just one.'

Then the mayor turned on his heel and walked back into the house. The door slammed behind him. Gretchen sadly left the window.

17

Now Jacob knew what to do.

He ran down the lane and blew his whistle. At once the man in red was by his side.

'What can I do for you ... Master?' he asked, smirking down at Jacob.

Jacob told him what the mayor had said. At once the stranger reached into his pocket. He brought out a tiny red plough and set it on the ground.

'Stand back,' he said.

The plough quickly grew to full size. Jacob was astonished. He turned to thank the stranger – but he was nowhere to be seen.

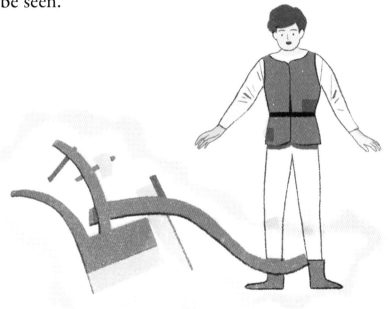

So Jacob put his hand out to touch the plough – and at once it began to move. It headed for Gretchen's house, ploughing all the way.

Jacob had to run to keep up. He was quite out of breath when he arrived at the mayor's house. Luckily the red plough stopped right outside the door. There were three straight furrows behind it. Gretchen blew Jacob a kiss from her window, then her father came out.

'Very good!' said the mayor, but there was a scowl on his face. He thought for a second.

'But I'm still not really sure you are worthy of my Gretchen,' he said. 'Have you got enough money? I can only let my daughter marry a man who always has money in his purse – no matter how much he takes out of it.'

And with a satisfied smile, he slammed the door on Jacob once again.

Gretchen watched sadly from the window as the young man walked away.

Jacob was angry. He'd done two impossible things, and still the mayor wouldn't budge! He had hardly gone round the corner before he blew the whistle again.

The red stranger was there at once. He was holding out a small red leather purse. Inside it were two gold coins.

'Take them out,' said the stranger.

Jacob did. The stranger shook the purse and Jacob heard coins clinking inside.

'Open it,' said the stranger.

There were still two gold coins inside!

Jacob took the purse and tried it again.

He took out two coins, then two more, and then another two.

He had a handful of coins now.

And when he looked, there were still two coins in the purse. This would impress the mayor indeed.

He was turning back
to the house when he
heard the stranger's
voice in his ear.

'I'll be coming for
you in ten years,'
it said.

Jacob knocked
on the mayor's
door, his pockets
jingling with money.
When Gretchen's
father appeared, Jacob
simply gave him the purse.

And while the mayor was piling up the
coins he took from the stranger's purse, and
finding every time that there were more still
inside, Gretchen ran out of the house and
kissed Jacob.

'I knew you were clever enough to beat him,' she whispered.

And so Jacob and Gretchen were married at last. They lived happily for nearly ten years. They ate well, thanks to Jacob's bow and plough, and always had enough money. But Jacob was starting to worry.

The night before the ten years were up, Jacob couldn't sleep. He tossed and turned, and at last went and sat by the fire.

Gretchen came after him. 'What's the matter?' she asked. 'I've never seen you so worried.'

So he told her all about the red stranger and the deal he had made. 'The stranger is always a step ahead of me. I could never think of a question he can't answer!' he said.

26

'I'll have to go and be his servant forever – and I can't bear to leave you!' Poor Jacob burst into tears.

Gretchen hugged Jacob, thinking hard. 'It won't come to that,' she said. She held his hand, and looked into the fire while she thought.

Then she told him her plan, and exactly what he should do the next day.

The next morning, Gretchen and Jacob were both up early. Jacob took his bow and sat outside the house, while Gretchen got busy inside.

She tore open a feather quilt and piled up all the feathers on the floor. Then she covered herself in honey from head to foot. Lastly, she jumped into the heap of feathers. She rolled around until they were stuck all over her.

'That should do it,' she said, and sneezed.

Suddenly Jacob realized that the stranger was sitting beside him. And he didn't look a day older than he had ten years before. Jacob felt a chill run down his spine.

'Come along,' said the stranger, and he waved the contract at Jacob. 'You've had your side of the deal; it's time for mine.'
Jacob got up as if to go with the stranger.

Then he picked up his bow, just as Gretchen had told him.

'This bow you fixed for me is the best thing ever,' he said. 'Can I use it one last time, before we go?'

'Of course,' smiled the stranger.

They walked to the edge of the woods. The stranger pointed out a raven. 'Will that do?' he asked.

'I don't want to shoot that – it's too black,' said Jacob.

The stranger sighed. 'All right, shoot that wren,' he said.

'No, that's too small,' said Jacob.

The stranger rolled his eyes.

'I know,' said Jacob, 'I'll shoot that!' He pointed to the fields by the wood, where a huge feathered creature was leaping about.

'Very well, get on with it,' said the stranger, tapping his foot on the ground.

Jacob raised his bow. 'What is it, though?' he asked.

'Who cares? It's time for you to come with me. Just shoot it!' said the stranger.

Jacob aimed at the creature. 'I'd really like to know, though,' he said, lowering his bow.

'Shoot and be done with it!'

Jacob looked the stranger straight in the eyes. 'Can you tell me what it is?' he asked.

'I don't know!' shouted the stranger. And at once he began to fade from sight.

With a hissing noise, he vanished in a twirl of red smoke. He hadn't been able to answer Jacob's question, so Jacob was free.

Jacob dropped his bow and ran into the field to thank his clever Gretchen. It took a lot of washing to get rid of the feathers and honey – but they did live happily ever after.

The Three Daughters – an African dilemma tale

Once there was a man who had three daughters. Each daughter owned a magical item. One had a mirror that could show her things that were many miles away. Another had a hammock that could take her anywhere in the blink of an eye. The third had a medicine that could cure any illness.

One day their father went out hunting. But he was very late coming home and his daughters started to worry.

The first daughter looked in her mirror. She saw their father lying on the ground, very ill.

The second daughter spread out her
hammock and they all climbed in. At once,
it took them to their father's side.

The third daughter opened her bottle of
medicine and poured it into his mouth.

In a few seconds, their father was well
again. He kissed all his daughters.

But which one should he be most
grateful to?

The Circle of Chalk

Many years ago, in China, there was a beautiful young woman called Haitang. She lived with her mother, father, brothers and sisters. They were never rich, but they were happy.

Then Haitang's father became ill. He couldn't work, and after a few months, he died. The family were very sad and now they were poor too.

'How will I feed all my children?' wept Haitang's mother. Haitang kissed her and dried her tears.

'Don't worry,' she said. 'I'm old enough to work. So I'll find a job and send you my wages.'

The very next day, Haitang put on her best clothes and went to the nearest town. The owner of the teahouse saw at once how beautiful she was and offered her a job.

The teahouse was a place
where people came
after work; to talk,
drink tea and
listen to music.
Haitang was not
only beautiful,
she also had a
lovely voice, so
her job was to sing
and dance. She soon got
to know the customers at
the teahouse and every week
she sent money home to her family.

One day, when Haitang had finished
performing, a man called Mr Ma asked her
to sit and talk with him. His smile was so
kind, she agreed at once. They talked until
the teahouse closed for the night.

Haitang's heart fluttered when she saw
Mr Ma watching and waiting for her the
next day. Soon she spent part of every day
talking with him. They were falling in love.

Eventually gentle Mr Ma asked
Haitang if she would marry him. He even
offered to send money to her mother.
Of course, Haitang said yes.

So Haitang left her job at the
teahouse and went to live with Mr Ma.
She already knew that his old wife still
lived in part of his house. Everyone
even carried on calling her Mrs Ma. But
Haitang wasn't expecting Mrs Ma to be
so jealous of her.

Wherever Haitang went in the house,
Mrs Ma was watching her. When she
went into the garden with Mr Ma,
Mrs Ma would come too. She sat so
close to them that Haitang felt shy and
unhappy with her own husband.
In fact, Haitang only really
relaxed when Mrs Ma went out.

After a while, Haitang became pregnant and had a baby son, who she named Shoulang. She and Mr Ma adored their son. They were so happy, Haitang stopped even noticing that Mrs Ma was there.

But Mrs Ma watched beautiful Haitang singing to her baby and her jealousy boiled over. She started plotting a horrible revenge.

One day, when Mr Ma was playing with Shoulang, he asked Haitang to get him a drink. Straight away, Mrs Ma came up and gave Haitang some tea she had made herself.

'You poor thing, you are so busy with the baby! Take this drink I made. No – you give it to him,' said Mrs Ma, when Haitang looked at her in surprise. 'After all, you are his wife.'

Haitang gave her husband the tea. Mr Ma drank it, and at once, he started to cough. He became so ill that he died that night. Mrs Ma had poisoned him!

The next morning, the town guards came to the house to find out what had happened. Mrs Ma fell on her knees in front of them.

'Haitang has stolen my husband and my little baby boy, Shoulang,' she lied. 'And now she has poisoned Mr Ma so she can have his money! I saw her give him a drink yesterday, and he got ill as soon as he drank it!'

The guards felt sorry for Mrs Ma, and believed her story. Haitang wept and clung to Shoulang, but they took him from her arms and gave him to Mrs Ma. Then they marched Haitang to prison.

At last the day came for the judge to decide what should happen to Haitang. Mrs Ma brought her servants to the court. They all swore that Shoulang was Mrs Ma's son, and that Haitang had made Mr Ma the poisoned drink. Out of her cell window, Haitang saw Mrs Ma giving the servants gold as they left the court, to pay them for lying.

But the judge was a wise man. He saw the spiteful way Mrs Ma looked at Haitang, and how nervous the servants were. He wasn't sure he should trust Mrs Ma.

'I need to find out who is really the boy's mother,' he decided. 'Then I will know who is telling the truth about the murder.'

But which woman was Shoulang's mother? Just as he was falling asleep that night, the judge had an idea. Now he knew how to answer the question.

***

The next day, the judge ordered a circle of chalk to be drawn on the courtroom floor.

'Put Shoulang in the chalk circle,' he told the guards.

Then he placed the two women on opposite sides of the circle.

'You must each hold one of his arms,' he ordered. 'When I say, you both pull – and whichever one of you pulls Shoulang out of the circle is his true mother. Now pull!'

At once, Mrs Ma yanked hard on Shoulang's arm, pulling the boy to her.

The judge could not believe how easily Mrs Ma had won – it looked as if Haitang wasn't trying.

'Again,' he said. 'You both need to pull.' He decided to watch more carefully this time, to see what was happening.

Again, Mrs Ma dragged Shoulang out of the circle. The judge saw that Haitang let go as soon as the other woman began to pull. And yet her eyes were full of tears. What was going on?

He put on a very stern expression – he had to make sure Haitang knew how serious the situation was.

'You must pull!' he said. 'Or I will have to send you to prison for murdering your husband!'

A third time they placed Shoulang in the circle. Haitang gently held his arm, while Mrs Ma seized the other one.

'Pull,' said the judge, and he watched Haitang even more closely than before.

Mrs Ma pulled roughly on Shoulang's arm, and Haitang let go as soon as she felt the tug. Her hand fell limply to her side and tears rolled down her face.

Now the wise judge understood that
Haitang was letting go on purpose –
and why.

'Mrs Ma,' he said, 'Give Haitang
her son.'

'No! He is *my* son!' shrieked Mrs Ma.
'I pulled him out of the circle – I passed
the test! She killed my husband!'

The judge nodded. 'Mrs Ma, you pulled him out because Haitang let you, every time. Tell me why, Haitang.'

Haitang looked up and spoke in a small voice. 'Mrs Ma pulled so hard, Shoulang's arm would break if I pulled too. I could not hurt my son.'

'That is why, Mrs Ma,' said the judge.
'His real mother could not bear to cause her
son such pain. She would rather have you
claim Shoulang and go to jail herself.
Now guards! Arrest Mrs Ma. She has lied
about this important fact, and I say she also
poisoned Mr Ma.'

Now Haitang pulled Shoulang to her and hugged her son tight. 'I'll never let you go again,' she whispered. They were set free, and Mrs Ma was sent to prison – thanks to the wise judge and the circle of chalk.